My TravelJournal

____

Date: | Place:

How I felt Today:

What I've Seen today:

____

____

____

____

____

____

____

____

____

What I Ate Today:

____

____

____

____

How did we Travel:

The Best Thing that happened tooday:

____

____

The Weather today was:

Place for Drawings, paintings, writing, entry tickets, pictures or all the other stuff you want to capture

Date: Place:

How I felt Today:

What I've Seen today:

____
____
____
____
____
____
____
____
____
____

What I Ate Today:

____
____
____
____
____

How did we Travel:

The Best Thing that happened tooday:

____
____

The Weather today was:

Place for Drawings, paintings, writing, entry tickets, pictures or all the other stuff you want to capture

Date: Place:

How I felt Today:

What I've Seen today:

____

____

____

____

____

____

____

____

____

____

____

What I Ate Today:

____

____

____

____

How did we Travel:

The Best Thing that happened tooday:

____

____

THe Weather today was:

Place for Drawings, paintings, writing, entry tickets, pictures or all the other stuff you want to capture

Date:

Place:

How I felt Today:

What I've Seen today:

____
____
____
____
____
____
____
____
____
____

What I Ate Today:

____
____
____
____

How did we Travel:

The Best Thing that happened tooday:

____
____

The Weather today was:

Place for Drawings, paintings, writing, entry tickets, pictures or all the other stuff you want to capture

Date: Place:

How I felt Today:

What I've Seen today:

____
____
____
____
____
____
____
____
____

What I Ate Today:

____
____
____
____

How did we Travel:

The Best Thing that happened tooday:
____
____

The Weather today was:

PLACE FOR DRAWINGS, PAINTINGS, WRITING, ENTRY TICKETS, PICTURES OR ALL THE OTHER STUFF YOU WANT TO CAPTURE

Date: Place:

How I felt Today:

What I've Seen today:

____
____
____
____
____
____
____
____
____
____

What I Ate Today:

____
____
____
____

How did we Travel:

The Best Thing that happened tooday:

____
____

THe Weather today was:

Place for Drawings, paintings, writing, entry tickets, pictures or all the other stuff you want to capture

DATE: PLACE:

HOW I FELT TODAY:

WHAT I'VE SEEN TODAY:

WHAT I ATE TODAY:

HOW DID WE TRAVEL:

THE BEST THING THAT HAPPENED TOODAY:

THE WEATHER TODAY WAS:

PLACE FOR DRAWINGS, PAINTINGS, WRITING, ENTRY TICKETS, PICTURES OR ALL THE OTHER STUFF YOU WANT TO CAPTURE

Date: | Place:

How I felt Today:

What I've Seen today:

____
____
____
____
____
____
____
____
____
____
____

What I Ate Today:

____
____
____
____
____

How did we Travel:

The Best Thing that happened Tooday:

____
____

The Weather today was:

Place for Drawings, paintings, writing, entry tickets, pictures or all the other stuff you want to capture

Date: Place:

How I felt Today:

What I've Seen today:

____

____

____

____

____

____

____

____

____

____

What I Ate Today:

____

____

____

____

How did we Travel:

The Best Thing that happened Tooday:

____

____

THe Weather today was:

Place for Drawings, paintings, writing, entry tickets, pictures or all the other stuff you want to capture

DATE: | PLACE:

HOW I FELT TODAY:

WHAT I'VE SEEN TODAY:

WHAT I ATE TODAY:

HOW DID WE TRAVEL:

THE BEST THING THAT HAPPENED TOODAY:

THE WEATHER TODAY WAS:

Place for Drawings, paintings, writing, entry tickets, pictures or all the other stuff you want to capture

Date: Place:

How I felt Today:

What I've Seen today:

____

____

____

____

____

____

____

____

____

____

What I Ate Today:

____

____

____

____

How did we Travel:

The Best Thing that happened tooday:

____

____

THe Weather today was:

Place for Drawings, paintings, writing, entry tickets, pictures or all the other stuff you want to capture

DATE: ________________ PLACE: ________________

HOW I FELT TODAY:

WHAT I'VE SEEN TODAY:

WHAT I ATE TODAY:

HOW DID WE TRAVEL:

THE BEST THING THAT HAPPENED TOODAY:

____

____

THE WEATHER TODAY WAS:

Place for Drawings, paintings, writing, entry tickets, pictures or all the other stuff you want to capture

DATE: | PLACE:

HOW I FELT TODAY:

WHAT I'VE SEEN TODAY:

WHAT I ATE TODAY:

HOW DID WE TRAVEL:

THE BEST THING THAT HAPPENED TOODAY:

THE WEATHER TODAY WAS:

Place for Drawings, paintings, writing, entry tickets, pictures or all the other stuff you want to capture

Date: ___________   Place: ___________

How I felt Today:

What I've Seen today:

____
____
____
____
____
____
____
____
____
____

What I Ate Today:

____
____
____
____
____

How did we Travel:

The Best Thing that happened tooday:

____
____

The Weather today was:

Place for Drawings, paintings, writing, entry tickets, pictures or all the other stuff you want to capture

Date: Place:

How I felt Today:

What I've Seen today:

What I Ate Today:

How did we Travel:

The Best Thing that happened Tooday:

The Weather today was:

Place for Drawings, paintings, writing, entry tickets, pictures or all the other stuff you want to capture

Date: Place:

How I felt Today:

What I've Seen today:

____

____

____

____

____

____

____

____

____

What I Ate Today:

____

____

____

____

How did we Travel:

The Best Thing that happened tooday:

____

____

The Weather today was:

Place for Drawings, paintings, writing, entry tickets, pictures or all the other stuff you want to capture

Date: Place:

How I felt Today:

What I've Seen today:

____

____

____

____

____

____

____

____

____

____

What I Ate Today:

____

____

____

____

____

How did we Travel:

The Best Thing that happened tooday:

____

____

The Weather today was:

Place for Drawings, paintings, writing, entry tickets, pictures or all the other stuff you want to capture

Date: Place:

How I felt Today:

What I've Seen today:

____

____

____

____

____

____

____

____

____

What I Ate Today:

____

____

____

____

How did we Travel:

The Best Thing that happened tooday:

____

____

THe Weather today was:

Place for Drawings, paintings, writing, entry tickets, pictures or all the other stuff you want to capture

Date: | Place:

How I felt Today:

What I've Seen today: | ## What I Ate Today:

How did we Travel:

The Best Thing that happened Tooday:

THe Weather today was:

PLACE FOR DRAWINGS, PAINTINGS, WRITING, ENTRY TICKETS, PICTURES OR ALL THE OTHER STUFF YOU WANT TO CAPTURE

Date: Place:

How I felt Today:

What I've Seen today:

____
____
____
____
____
____
____
____
____

What I Ate Today:

____
____
____
____

How did we Travel:

The Best Thing that happened tooday:

____
____

THe Weather today was:

Place for Drawings, paintings, writing, entry tickets, pictures or all the other stuff you want to capture

Date: Place:

How I felt Today:

What I've Seen today:

____
____
____
____
____
____
____
____
____
____

What I Ate Today:

____
____
____
____

How did we Travel:

The Best Thing that happened Tooday:
____
____

THe Weather today was:

Place for Drawings, paintings, writing, entry tickets, pictures or all the other stuff you want to capture

Date: Place:

How I felt Today:

What I've Seen today:

____
____
____
____
____
____
____
____
____
____

What I Ate Today:

____
____
____
____

How did we Travel:

The Best Thing that happened tooday:

____
____

The Weather today was:

Place for Drawings, paintings, writing, entry tickets, pictures or all the other stuff you want to capture

Date: Place:

How I felt Today:

What I've Seen today:

____

____

____

____

____

____

____

____

____

____

____

What I Ate Today:

____

____

____

____

How did we Travel:

The Best Thing that happened Tooday:

____

____

THe Weather today was:

PLACE FOR DRAWINGS, PAINTINGS, WRITING, ENTRY TICKETS, PICTURES OR ALL THE OTHER STUFF YOU WANT TO CAPTURE

Date: Place:

How I felt Today:

What I've Seen today: What I Ate Today:

_______________________________   _______________________________

_______________________________   _______________________________

_______________________________   _______________________________

_______________________________   _______________________________

____

_______________________________   How did we Travel:

____

____

____

The Best Thing that happened tooday:

____

____

THe Weather today was:

Place for Drawings, paintings, writing, entry tickets, pictures or all the other stuff you want to capture

Date: Place:

How I felt Today:

What I've Seen today:

____
____
____
____
____
____
____
____
____
____
____

What I Ate Today:

____
____
____
____

How did we Travel:

The Best Thing that happened Tooday:

____
____

THe Weather today was:

Place for Drawings, paintings, writing, entry tickets, pictures or all the other stuff you want to capture

Date: Place:

How I felt Today:

What I've Seen today:

____
____
____
____
____
____
____
____
____
____

What I Ate Today:

____
____
____
____

How did we Travel:

The Best Thing that happened Tooday:

____
____

The Weather today was:

Place for Drawings, paintings, writing, entry tickets, pictures or all the other stuff you want to capture

Date: Place:

How I felt Today:

What I've Seen today:

____

____

____

____

____

____

____

____

____

____

What I Ate Today:

____

____

____

____

How did we Travel:

The Best Thing that happened tooday:

____

____

The Weather today was:

Place for Drawings, paintings, writing, entry tickets, pictures or all the other stuff you want to capture

Date: | Place:

How I felt Today:

What I've Seen today:

____
____
____
____
____
____
____
____
____
____

What I Ate Today:

____
____
____
____

How did we Travel:

The Best Thing that happened tooday:

____
____

The Weather today was:

Place for Drawings, paintings, writing, entry tickets, pictures or all the other stuff you want to capture

Date: Place:

How I felt Today:

What I've Seen today:

____

____

____

____

____

____

____

____

____

____

What I Ate Today:

____

____

____

____

How did we Travel:

The Best Thing that happened tooday:

____

____

THe Weather today was:

Place for Drawings, paintings, writing, entry tickets, pictures or all the other stuff you want to capture

DATE: | PLACE:

HOW I FELT TODAY:

WHAT I'VE SEEN TODAY:

WHAT I ATE TODAY:

HOW DID WE TRAVEL:

THE BEST THING THAT HAPPENED TOODAY:

THE WEATHER TODAY WAS:

Place for Drawings, paintings, writing, entry tickets, pictures or all the other stuff you want to capture

Date:
Place:

How I felt Today:

What I've Seen today:

What I Ate Today:

How did we Travel:

The Best Thing that happened tooday:

The Weather today was:

Place for Drawings, paintings, writing, entry tickets, pictures or all the other stuff you want to capture

Date: Place:

How I felt Today:

What I've Seen today:

What I Ate Today:

How did we Travel:

The Best Thing that happened tooday:

THe Weather today was:

Place for Drawings, paintings, writing, entry tickets, pictures or all the other stuff you want to capture

Date: Place:

How I felt Today:

What I've Seen today:

____
____
____
____
____
____
____
____
____
____
____

What I Ate Today:

____
____
____
____

How did we Travel:

The Best Thing that happened tooday:

____
____

THe Weather today was:

Place for Drawings, paintings, writing, entry tickets, pictures or all the other stuff you want to capture

Date: Place:

How I felt Today:

What I've Seen today:

____
____
____
____
____
____
____
____
____
____
____

What I Ate Today:

____
____
____
____

How did we Travel:

The Best Thing that happened Tooday:

____
____

The Weather today was:

Place for Drawings, paintings, writing, entry tickets, pictures or all the other stuff you want to capture

Date: Place:

How I felt Today:

What I've Seen today:

____
____
____
____
____
____
____
____
____
____

What I Ate Today:

____
____
____
____

How did we Travel:

The Best Thing that happened tooday:

____
____

THe Weather today was:

Place for Drawings, paintings, writing, entry tickets, pictures or all the other stuff you want to capture

DATE: | PLACE:

HOW I FELT TODAY:

WHAT I'VE SEEN TODAY:

WHAT I ATE TODAY:

HOW DID WE TRAVEL:

THE BEST THING THAT HAPPENED TOODAY:

THE WEATHER TODAY WAS:

Place for Drawings, paintings, writing, entry tickets, pictures or all the other stuff you want to capture

Date: Place:

How I felt Today:

What I've Seen today:

____

____

____

____

____

____

____

____

____

____

What I Ate Today:

____

____

____

____

How did we Travel:

The Best Thing that happened Tooday:

____

____

THe Weather today was:

Place for Drawings, paintings, writing, entry tickets, pictures or all the other stuff you want to capture

Date: Place:

How I felt Today:

What I've Seen today:

____

____

____

____

____

____

____

____

____

____

____

What I Ate Today:

____

____

____

____

How did we Travel:

The Best Thing that happened tooday:

____

____

THe Weather today was:

PLACE FOR DRAWINGS, PAINTINGS, WRITING, ENTRY TICKETS, PICTURES OR ALL THE OTHER STUFF YOU WANT TO CAPTURE

Date: Place:

How I felt Today:

What I've Seen today:

____

____

____

____

____

____

____

____

____

____

What I Ate Today:

____

____

____

How did we Travel:

The Best Thing that happened tooday:

____

____

The Weather today was:

PLACE FOR DRAWINGS, PAINTINGS, WRITING, ENTRY TICKETS, PICTURES OR ALL THE OTHER STUFF YOU WANT TO CAPTURE

Date: | Place:

How I felt Today:

What I've Seen today:

What I Ate Today:

How did we Travel:

The Best Thing that happened tooday:

THe Weather today was:

Place for Drawings, paintings, writing, entry tickets, pictures or all the other stuff you want to capture

DATE: PLACE:

HOW I FELT TODAY:

WHAT I'VE SEEN TODAY:

WHAT I ATE TODAY:

HOW DID WE TRAVEL:

THE BEST THING THAT HAPPENED TOODAY:

THE WEATHER TODAY WAS:

Place for Drawings, paintings, writing, entry tickets, pictures or all the other stuff you want to capture

Date: .... Place: ....

How I felt Today:

What I've Seen today:

____
____
____
____
____
____
____
____
____
____
____

What I Ate Today:

____
____
____
____

How did we Travel:

The Best Thing that happened tooday:

____
____

THe Weather today was:

Place for Drawings, paintings, writing, entry tickets, pictures or all the other stuff you want to capture

Date: Place:

How I felt Today:

What I've Seen today:

____

____

____

____

____

____

____

____

____

____

What I Ate Today:

____

____

____

____

How did we Travel:

The Best Thing that happened Tooday:

____

____

The Weather today was:

Place for Drawings, paintings, writing, entry tickets, pictures or all the other stuff you want to capture

Date: Place:

How I felt Today:

What I've Seen today:

____

____

____

____

____

____

____

____

____

____

What I Ate Today:

____

____

____

____

How did we Travel:

The Best Thing that happened tooday:

____

____

THe Weather today was:

Place for Drawings, paintings, writing, entry tickets, pictures or all the other stuff you want to capture

Date: Place:

How I felt Today:

What I've Seen today:

____

____

____

____

____

____

____

____

____

____

What I Ate Today:

____

____

____

____

How did we Travel:

The Best Thing that happened tooday:

____

____

THe Weather today was:

Place for Drawings, paintings, writing, entry tickets, pictures or all the other stuff you want to capture

Date: Place:

How I felt Today:

What I've Seen today:

____

____

____

____

____

____

____

____

____

____

What I Ate Today:

____

____

____

____

How did we Travel:

The Best Thing that happened tooday:

____

____

The Weather today was:

Place for Drawings, paintings, writing, entry tickets, pictures or all the other stuff you want to capture

Date: | Place:

How I felt Today:

What I've Seen today: | What I Ate Today:

____

How did we Travel:

The Best Thing that happened Tooday:

____

THe Weather today was:

Place for Drawings, paintings, writing, entry tickets, pictures or all the other stuff you want to capture

Date: Place:

How I felt Today:

What I've Seen today:

____

____

____

____

____

____

____

____

What I Ate Today:

____

____

____

How did we Travel:

The Best Thing that happened tooday:

____

____

THe Weather today was:

Place for Drawings, paintings, writing, entry tickets, pictures or all the other stuff you want to capture

Date: Place:

How I felt Today:

What I've Seen today: What I Ate Today:

_______________________   _______________________

_______________________   _______________________

_______________________   _______________________

_______________________   _______________________

_______________________   _______________________

____

_______________________   How did we Travel:

____

____

The Best Thing that happened tooday:

____

____

The Weather today was:

Place for Drawings, paintings, writing, entry tickets, pictures or all the other stuff you want to capture

Date: Place:

How I felt Today:

What I've Seen today: What I Ate Today:

_______________________   _______________________

_______________________   _______________________

_______________________   _______________________

_______________________   _______________________

_______________________   _______________________

_______________________   How did we Travel:

____

____

____

____

The Best Thing that happened tooday:

____

____

THe Weather today was:

PLACE FOR DRAWINGS, PAINTINGS, WRITING, ENTRY TICKETS, PICTURES OR ALL THE OTHER STUFF YOU WANT TO CAPTURE

DATE: PLACE:

HOW I FELT TODAY:

WHAT I'VE SEEN TODAY:

WHAT I ATE TODAY:

HOW DID WE TRAVEL:

THE BEST THING THAT HAPPENED TOODAY:

THE WEATHER TODAY WAS:

Place for Drawings, paintings, writing, entry tickets, pictures or all the other stuff you want to capture

Date: | Place:

How I felt Today:

What I've Seen today:

____

____

____

____

____

____

____

____

____

What I Ate Today:

____

____

____

____

How did we Travel:

The Best Thing that happened tooday:

____

____

The Weather today was:

Place for Drawings, paintings, writing, entry tickets, pictures or all the other stuff you want to capture

Date: Place:

How I felt Today:

What I've Seen today:

What I Ate Today:

How did we Travel:

The Best Thing that happened tooday:

THe Weather today was:

Place for Drawings, paintings, writing, entry tickets, pictures or all the other stuff you want to capture

Date: | Place:

How I felt Today:

What I've Seen today:

____

____

____

____

____

____

____

____

____

____

What I Ate Today:

____

____

____

____

____

How did we Travel:

The Best Thing that happened Tooday:

____

____

The Weather today was:

Place for Drawings, paintings, writing, entry tickets, pictures or all the other stuff you want to capture

Date: Place:

How I felt Today:

What I've Seen today:

____

____

____

____

____

____

____

____

____

What I Ate Today:

____

____

____

____

How did we Travel:

The Best Thing that happened tooday:

____

____

The Weather today was:

Place for Drawings, paintings, writing, entry tickets, pictures or all the other stuff you want to capture

Date: Place:

How I felt Today:

What I've Seen today:

____
____
____
____
____
____
____
____
____
____

What I Ate Today:

____
____
____
____

How did we Travel:

The Best Thing that happened tooday:

____
____

THe Weather today was:

Place for Drawings, paintings, writing, entry tickets, pictures or all the other stuff you want to capture

Date: Place:

How I felt Today:

What I've Seen today:

What I Ate Today:

How did we Travel:

The Best Thing that happened tooday:

THe Weather today was:

Place for Drawings, paintings, writing, entry tickets, pictures or all the other stuff you want to capture

Date: _______________   Place: _______________

How I felt Today:

How I've Seen today:

____
____
____
____
____
____
____
____
____
____
____

What I Ate Today:

____
____
____
____
____

How did we Travel:

The Best Thing that happened tooday:

____
____

The Weather today was:

Place for Drawings, paintings, writing, entry tickets, pictures or all the other stuff you want to capture

Date: | Place:

How I felt Today:

What I've Seen today:

____
____
____
____
____
____
____
____
____

What I Ate Today:

____
____
____
____

How did we Travel:

The Best Thing that happened tooday:

____
____

THe Weather today was:

Place for Drawings, paintings, writing, entry tickets, pictures or all the other stuff you want to capture